DROUGHTS

by Jaclyn Jaycox

PEBBLE
a capstone imprint

Published by Pebble, an imprint of Capstone
1710 Roe Crest Drive, North Mankato, Minnesota 56003
capstonepub.com

Copyright © 2022 by Capstone. All rights reserved. No part of this publication may be reproduced in whole or in part, or stored in a retrieval system, or transmitted in any form or by any means, electronic, mechanical, photocopying, recording, or otherwise, without written permission of the publisher.

Library of Congress Cataloging-in-Publication Data
Names: Jaycox, Jaclyn, 1983- author.
Title: Droughts / by Jaclyn Jaycox.
Description: North Mankato, Minnesota : Pebble, [2022] | Series: Wild earth science | Includes bibliographical references and index. | Audience: Ages 5-8 | Audience: Grades K-1 |
Summary: "Dry land. Thirsty plants. When rains don't come, droughts happen. Desert, forest, or prairies-droughts can happen anywhere. Discover how small shifts in rain amounts can cause big changes to the land. Learn about droughts, what causes them, and how living things adapt to survive"-- Provided by publisher.
Identifiers: LCCN 2021042158 (print) | LCCN 2021042159 (ebook) |
  ISBN 9781663977038 (hardcover) | ISBN 9781666327397 (paperback) |
  ISBN 9781666327403 (pdf) | ISBN 9781666327427 (kindle edition)
Subjects: LCSH: Droughts--Juvenile literature.
Classification: LCC QC929.25 .J39 2022 (print) | LCC QC929.25 (ebook) | DDC 551.57/73--dc23
LC record available at https://lccn.loc.gov/2021042158
LC ebook record available at https://lccn.loc.gov/2021042159)

Editorial Credits
Editor: Ericka Smith; Designer: Tracy Davies; Media Researcher: Svetlana Zhurkin; Production Specialist: Katy LaVigne

Image Credits
Newscom: Reuters/Thomas Mukoya, 15, Universal Images Group/Liszt Collection, 11; Shutterstock: almaje, 29, ArtMari, 17, Dan4Earth, 8, Deborah Kolb, 23, Dmitry Pichugin, 21, dynamic (map background), back cover and throughout, Erlo Brown, 9, John D Sirlin, 18, Johnny Habell, 19, Jon_Clark, cover, 3, Juice Flair, 1, 13, Kunal Mehta, 7, Mike Hardiman, 27, Nikola Barbutov, 25, nvelichko, 4, pashabo, cover (logo), Prometheus72, 5, sculler, 12, Sundraw Photography, 6, TinnaPong, 28, Wolf Avni, 26, xuanhuongho, 20

All internet sites appearing in back matter were available and accurate when this book was sent to press.

Printed and bound in China. PO# 5340

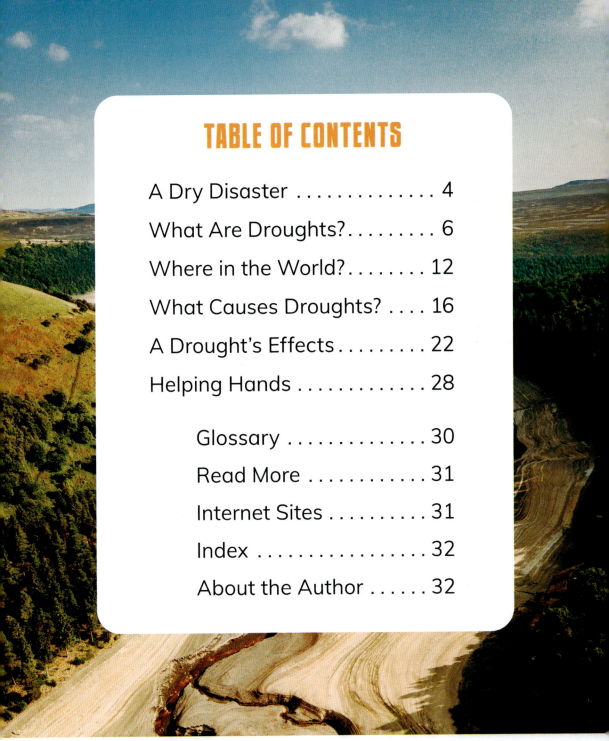

TABLE OF CONTENTS

A Dry Disaster 4

What Are Droughts? 6

Where in the World? 12

What Causes Droughts? 16

A Drought's Effects 22

Helping Hands 28

Glossary 30

Read More 31

Internet Sites 31

Index 32

About the Author 32

Words in **bold** are in the glossary.

A DRY DISASTER

It hasn't rained in months. The ground is dry and cracked. The grass is brown. Plants are dying. Animals have moved away. There isn't enough food and water. What could cause this? A drought!

A farmer in a field of dry crops in Turkey

Droughts are a natural **disaster**. They are harmful to people. They affect more people than any other natural disaster. They are harmful to plants and animals too.

WHAT ARE DROUGHTS?

A drought is when there is less **precipitation** than normal. It causes a water **shortage**. These dry conditions last a long time. A drought can last months. It might even last years.

Rain is one type of precipitation.

Severe drought caused Lake Mead in Nevada to lower by 140 feet (43 meters).

The worst droughts are called megadroughts. Megadroughts last 20 years or more.

Water levels decrease slowly.

Droughts happen differently than many other natural disasters. They don't have a clear start. They happen slowly. Weeks or months might pass before we know a drought is happening. They are hard to **predict**.

The end of a drought can happen slowly too. Lakes and rivers must fill up again. The ground must **absorb** water. It can take months of rain to end a drought.

Droughts can be dangerous. People need to drink water to survive. They also need it to grow food. Severe droughts can lead to **famine**. Famine is when there isn't enough food.

In the late 1870s, a horrible drought hit South America, Africa, and Asia. Crops died. This led to famine in many countries. Some estimate between 30 and 60 million people died.

People receiving rice in India during the 1870s drought

WHERE IN THE WORLD?

Droughts happen all over the world. But some places are at a higher risk. Areas with hot, dry weather are more likely to have droughts.

In these areas, water **evaporates** more quickly. So the land dries up fast.

Many places have had droughts recently. East Africa had a drought in 2011. It led to a famine. Tens of thousands of people died.

The southwestern United States had a drought from 2000 to 2018. It was the driest period there since the 1500s.

Families had to leave their homes during the drought in East Africa in 2011.

WHAT CAUSES DROUGHTS?

About 71 percent of Earth is covered with water. The water is always moving. This is called the water cycle.

First, the sun heats up the water. It evaporates and floats into the sky. Then, it forms into clouds.

Winds move the clouds around. The clouds become too full of water. Rain or snow falls. Water soaks into Earth's surface.

The water cycle

The water cycle keeps water moving around Earth. Each area has an **average** amount of rainfall. When there is less rain than normal, droughts can happen.

Drought dries out a field in California.

Changes to our **climate** affect the water cycle. The world is heating up. Water evaporates faster. Dry places are getting drier. They become more likely to have droughts.

Trees store water that helps the water cycle. But people cut down forests. That means less water in the water cycle. In this way, humans can contribute to droughts.

Trees that have been cut down in Vietnam

Watering crops grown in a desert

Humans also use too much water at times. We take it out of rivers. We use it to water crops. We use it to create electricity. This lowers the water levels.

A DROUGHT'S EFFECTS

Water is a part of our daily lives. We drink it and use it to grow food. We use it to wash clothes. We use it to wash dishes. And we swim in pools on hot days.

When there is not enough water, it affects many things. It needs to be used carefully.

Droughts affect about 55 million people each year. Clean water may be harder to find during droughts. People may be forced to drink dirty water. They may also have to use dirty water for bathing and cooking. This can make people very sick.

Droughts impact our food too. Farmers can't grow crops without water. Fewer crops means less food. This causes food prices to rise. Some people aren't able to **afford** the food they need.

Droughts can destroy crops.

Droughts harm plants and animals too. Plants need water to live. Animals need water to drink. And many of them eat plants for food. Some may leave to find food and water. Those that stay may not survive.

Droughts can lead to other natural disasters. They can cause wildfires. Dry, dead trees burn more easily. Droughts can also cause flooding. Rain from a sudden storm won't soak into dry ground. It just runs off.

HELPING HANDS

The climate is changing. The world is warming. And droughts are happening more often. But we can do some things to help.

During a drought, **conserving** water is key. You can help do that. Take shorter showers. Turn the water off while brushing your teeth. Try not to dump water down the drain. Use it to water plants instead. Small changes can make a difference.

GLOSSARY

absorb (ab-ZORB}—to soak up

afford (uh-FORD)—to be able to pay for something

average (AV-uh-rij)—being the usual amount of something

climate (KLY-muht)—the average weather of a place throughout the year

conserve (kuhn-SURV)—to protect something from being wasted or lost

disaster (dih-ZASS-tuhr)—an event that causes much damage or suffering

evaporate (ee-VAP-or-ayt)—to change from a liquid into a vapor or a gas

famine (FA-muhn)—a lack of food that causes widespread hunger and death

precipitation (pri-sip-ih-TAY-shuhn)—water that falls from the clouds in the form of rain, hail, or snow

predict (pri-DIKT)—to say what you think will happen in the future

shortage (SHOR-tij)—a situation in which there is not enough of something needed

READ MORE

London, Martha. *Droughts*. Minneapolis: Pop!, 2020.

Peterson, Megan Cooley. *Understanding Weather*. North Mankato, MN: Capstone Press, 2021.

Pettiford, Rebecca. *Droughts*. Minneapolis: Bellwether Media, 2020.

INTERNET SITES

Kiddle: "Drought Facts for Kids"
kids.kiddle.co/Drought#Causes_of_drought

The Conversation: "Curious Kids: Why Do We Have a Drought?"
theconversation.com/curious-kids-why-do-we-have-a-drought-110592

Weather Wiz Kids: "Drought"
weatherwizkids.com/?page_id=89

INDEX

Africa, 10
  East Africa, 14
animals, 4, 5, 26
Asia, 10

climate change, 19, 28
clouds, 16
conserving, 29
crops, 10, 21, 24

famines, 10, 14
farmers, 24

lakes, 9

natural disasters, 5, 8, 27
  floods, 27
  megadroughts, 7
  wildfires, 27

plants, 4, 5, 26, 29
  trees, 20, 27
precipitation, 6
  rain, 4, 9, 16, 18, 27
rivers, 9, 21

South America, 10

United States, 14

water cycle, 16, 18–20

ABOUT THE AUTHOR

Jaclyn Jaycox is a children's book author and editor. When she's not writing, she loves reading and spending time with her family. She lives in southern Minnesota with her husband, two kids, and a spunky goldendoodle.